she: robed and wordless

she: robed and wordless

poems

lou ella hickman

Press 53
Winston-Salem

Press 53, LLC
PO Box 30314
Winston-Salem, NC 27130

First Edition

A TOM LOMBARDO POETRY SELECTION

Cover design by Kevin Morgan Watson

Cover art, "Children of Haiti," Copyright © 2012,
by Sister Marilyn Springs, I.W.B.S.,
used by permission of the artist.

Printed on acid-free paper
ISBN 978-1-941209-25-7

for my mother, who sang

acknowledgments

The author wishes to acknowlwdge the editors of the following publications in which the following poems first appeared:

"eve's lament," *Spirit*, vol. 59, 1994

"the woman with the hemorrhage," *Review for Religious*, May/June 1989

"hannah," *Anna's Journal*, June 1996 vol. 2, no. 1

"wife of jairus," *Sisters Today*, September 1990

"prodigal's mother," *Desert Call*, Summer 1987

"sarah talks to isaac," *Forefront*, Winter 1994

"leah," *First Things*, November 1993

"women bent with infirmity," *First Things*, December 2009

"abishag the shunammite," *The Bible Today*, May 1989 (as "King David and Abishag the Shummanite")

"bathsheba," *The Bible Today*, January 1988

"cure of the daughter of the canaanite woman," *The Bible Today*, May 1989

"martha," *Emmanuel*, December 1992

"elizabeth," *Emmanuel*, December 1992

"peter's mother-in-law," *Emmanuel*, December 1992

"mary," *Emmanuel*, December 1992

"hagar," *Judi-isms: From Adam to Zipporah*, 1991

"rebekah," *Judi-isms: From Adam to Zipporah*, 1991

"the wife and daughter of jephthah," *Judi-isms: From Adam to Zipporah*, 1991

"ruth," *Judi-isms: From Adam to Zipporah*, 1991

"she/winter," *Phoenix*, v. X, 1989

"the woman who washed Jesus' feet: resurrection monologue," *The Other Side*, March/April 1999 (This poem was also part of two art exhibits: 1992, sponsored by The International Registry for Religious Wo/Men Artists; 1999 Memorials, Sacred Spaces and Holy, sponsored by the Christian Fine Arts Association and South Fellowship, Denver, CO.)

"delilah's song," *Lucid Stone*, Winter 2001 #28

"the women of bethlehem: the slaughter of the innocents," *National Catholic Reporter*, December 19, 2003

"veronica wipes the face of Jesus," *Commonweal*, April 8, 2011

"a woman at the last supper," *America*, April 11, 2011

"the wife of matthew," *Vocations & Prayer*, April-June 2012

"one of Jesus' companions comments on the rich young man," *Vocations & Prayer*, July-Sept. 2012

"widow of naim," *Vineyards*, Vol. 3, Fall 2013 (online)

"mary magdalene," *Vocations and Prayer*, April June 2014

"widow of zarephath," *Commonweal*, June 1, 2014

"slave girl cured," *Pilgrim: A Journal of Catholic Experience*, Pentecost/Assumption 2014 (online)

"lydia: the dealer in purple goods," *Vocations and Prayer*, July-Sept 2014

contents

...was the Word...

Poets are porters. They open doors to new experiences that, if tasted deeply and embraced, have the power to transform our lives. Through the instrumentality of words and the dexterity of the imagination, poets give us access to aspects of life that, previous to a particular verse, were unspoken or unseen. For that ministry of deepening and broadening our life through the opening of doors, we should be grateful.

In *she: robed and wordless*, Sister Lou Ella invites us to reflect on biblical women who encountered grace and sins, joys and sorrows, life and death. Employing the facility or reverent empathy and the gift of language, this poet opens up for us what *might* have transpired in the minds and hearts of these feminine scriptural characters. We hear Sarah whisper that she sees ". . .other stars behind your silence," and Rebekah exclaim: "boys will be boys i suppose/ but did they have to start so soon/ my womb a battleground," and Rahab the prostitute tells how she lived, ". . . on the edge of things." We are taken into the monologues of the prodigal's mother who saved buttons to mend her son's favorite shirt and the woman caught in adultery who felt "condemned to a misery of silence," and the wife of Nicodemus who bemoans how "the hours sit on their hands between the meals i serve." It is obvious that these poems arise out of quiet prayer. It is obvious that a feminine voice gives compassionate expression to a variety of feminine experiences.

While many of the poems deal with serious issues (Hagar's rejection, the rape of Tamar, the innocents' slaughter), Sister Lou Ella brings a keen sense of humor to her poetry. In a verse dealing with the mother of the sons of Zebedee, we are taken into the motives of a scheming woman seeking high honors for her boys. Then we hear Peter's mother-in-law respond with sarcasm at hearing Peter called rock. In "hannah," dizzy, dazzling bring laughter to heart.

In the end, *she: robed and wordless* will provide a new and different platform to read about the women in the Bible. St. Ignatius, so fond of encouraging his followers to use their imagination in plumbing the depth of Biblical stories, would appreciate this volume. Each verse invites us to return to the story out of which they have arisen. And moving from verse to story, we may well find ourselves in prayer, a prayer that unites us in the communion of saints, so many of whom are spoken in this poetic volume.

Bishop Robert Morneau
Auxiliary Bishop of Green Bay, Retired

introduction

After Eve, who is the next woman named in the Bible?

That was the question I asked Lou Ella Hickman after I read a small sample of her poems that became the core of this collection. The poems in that sample were lovely lyrics in the voices of a few women who happened to be characters in Biblical stories.

She and I discussed how very interesting it would be to read an entire collection featuring the voices of the women from the Bible. Who were these women? What were their thoughts beyond the happenings on the pages? What were their struggles to make sense of their circumstances, to make sense of the men they lived with, and most importantly, to make sense of their deep and profound feelings?

Lou Ella Hickman—already a widely published poet and Catholic nun—took a few years to produce *she: robed and wordless* to give the ordinary, often unseen women the chance to speak, and these poems reveal extraordinary women.

There are heroines like Judith and Mary. There are also women with darker motives like Bathsheba and Delilah. There are prostitutes and spies, queens and paupers. There are victims like Tamar. There are countless long-suffering wives and mothers, most unnamed, like Lot's wife and daughters, the mother of Peter and Andrew, the waitress at the Last Supper, the woman with a hemorrhage, the wives and mothers of people risen from the dead, and many others.

You may know some of these stories. Now, in this collection, you will discover what these women may have been thinking as watershed events took place around them in the stories from a book that may be the most studied, most revered, and yet most controversial book in Western literature.

Sister Lou Ella (as she prefers to be called) delves deeply into the souls of these women and hears the voices of the Feminine hidden in the shadows of the men who surround them.

She has revisited—and perhaps improved upon— the theme of Carol Ann Duffy, the current poet laureate of the United Kingdom, in her collection *The World's Wife*, a poetic peek into the lives of the wives of famous men through history. As Duffy has done, Sister Lou Ella imagines beyond the literal to the figurative muse of her women.

The question I posed at the outset revealed its importance to me when I tested it on two seminary professors of my acquaintance, one of them a Biblical scholar. Each of them gave uncomprehending looks, and I could tell their inner wheels were turning. One pulled out his cell phone and used his Bible app to scan the Book of Genesis. This gave me a very strong sense that Sister Lou Ella might be onto something important.

After Eve, there proceed millennia of begetting and begatting—millennia of the screams of anonymous women in labor—where the fathers and sons are named. And named. And named. And then comes along Sarah, the second woman who's given a name and a personality. She was the wife of Abraham, who is the figurative father of monotheism. Sarah, who was barren for decades, eventually bore a son to Abraham in her old age, and then she stood by helplessly as Abraham prepared to sacrifice her son to an insistent God as proof of his faith. You may have heard this story. Now, Sister Lou Ella Hickman will enlighten you as to how Sarah may have felt about it.

You may agree with me that the voices of Eve, of Sarah, of their sisters throughout the Bible could well be the same voices we might hear among twenty-first-century women as we beget and begat our way to our future. And readers might contemplate a new question posed by *she: robed and wordless*: How much has changed in the lives of creation's women?

Tom Lombardo
Poetry Series Editor

prologue: she/winter

dark like some shy wolf

came and she was robed wordless

...a forest and snow

In the beginning . . .

creation: the Spirit speaks

let me set the record straight
and I will be brief—
 creation
from nothing
would have been the first magic trick
                    instead
          my fiery breath
               hovered
     over the dark waters of the abyss

the name *woman* speaks to those who are abused

epic was the fabric of his storytelling
        and i, often an invisible thread ...
it was at the beginning he named me
        woven into my soul—
                yours
        remember that and not be ashamed

bone of my bones and flesh of my flesh

first love, first love song ...there you are—
standing before me reflection of strength,
weakness and with everything in between
bone   source of blood   flinty fire flesh
     and such a voice
     for such a first love song
      such a first love
       every love song since
       there you are standing before me

eve: the tree of knowledge

it grew within us
a wall
a living thing
from silent seed
and for its sap—a mortar
brick by brick
each a leaf
until the deadly fruit
out of poisoned flowers
ripened, plucked
then in each of us
the child died

on this wall
a terrible altar
to an unknown god

eve's lament

a curse is now my skin
his bitterness plows the earth
cain's mark was also mine
every shame is carried like a dead child
now we the thistles which briar everything

after eve...then what?

like words spoken once
    then forgotten
we lived
    we lived in the ordinary
        wives, mothers, sisters...
    a world whose honor or shame would lie
        in what was begotten
    countless as words in books
we, the paradox of the obvious, the mundane
    words nameless as the dust
    flaming each sunset and sunrise
        a thousand years more

sarah

i am she who wears a gown of skin
        velvet beneath your touch and weight
you call me evening and that is who i am—
i who offer myrrh among my hair
                a tent of meeting your embrace
yet
who am i
        the answers will come mingled in the sand
as this reckless journey still hungers in your voice
for i who follow you
                see other stars behind your silence
i who also hunger to linger at your silken sleeve

lot's daughter speaks about her mother

now
        in looking back i realize mother
lived in whispers always whispering
her longing for a place to call home
        more than longing for children she longed
and sighed until she got her way
only to disappear in her leaving
where she still whispers

lot's daughter

i am a good girl, really...
    raised on virtue, taught that honor mattered
      but life—precious, fragile, and rare...
          whatever the cost, i'll pay
          now,
            it is the wine that matters
            and it will bear fruit in me

hagar

she simply said *go*
and so i went
out into the morning's light with a sleeping child
our pain so wild
our battles will never end

sarah talks to isaac

what memories do you have,
my son
of fire and wood
        of soft thunder from the sky
        proclaiming blessing

when you look at brambles
what do you feel my laughing child
now a silent man

what are wool and ropes
sharp edges as you work—
nothing more than tools to your strong hands

memories become the man
your father blessed with
everything
it seemed so unfair
yet you the blessing
a thousand fold
waited, waited for
until the desert blossomed mirth
        and i was woman again
          to give you birth

13

rebekah

boys will be boys i suppose
but did they have to start so soon
my womb a battleground

nights i could not sleep—
for a universe of quarreling

        we must have sons my husband prayed
        what is life without them he would weep
        but he did not carry armies
         within a tomb of darkness
         and he did not wail until the dawn
         to birth a plea with divinity

rachel

just once he spoke of it—
  and just once was far too many
        i cannot bear to see again
those splintered edges of glass
which shone for eyes
then
      for our pillow and our night
      he clung to a thousand-eyed blessing in disguise

leah

how was it that he would want to earn her
a second wife

desire
        the way he would shear at my father's sheep

            every muscle bent
            and his neck throbbing

        a hidden sun from some distant blessing

  desire
        even as he ate the food i would prepare   with
        his fingers held mid air
                at times
                the only talking between us

how was it then
        into our nights where
everything practical
        measured became
        for every son i bore him
        the war i could never win

miriam, the prophetess, dances with her people
    at the red sea

the water parted
we are the miracle
                    the water parted we saw
        the chariots   we dance we are the
        miracle
                we saw
            the water
                    the miracle
                        the dance

rahab: prostitute of jericho

like every other woman in my profession
  i was somebody's daughter once
  now i am a daughter of israel
  a good story, really...
they came
     strangers, intense about a strange, intense god
     wanting to know who was who in the city
     then i did what i knew best—
       i made a deal...
  now, i who was on the edge of things
      and they, the strangers
    know more than most
    the kinship of promise:
         the cord that binds

the wife and daughter of jephthah

for the last few nights i've heard her
late night or early morning
as i cannot sleep in my loss of her
she wails for she knows her womb is cold
her passion frozen like the killing frost we had last winter

     my rage a killing frost

delilah's song

bring the perfume of your wanderings
and anoint my breast to pillow your lonely head
let the dark orchard between my thighs refresh
the ancient land of you waiting
then drunk with dance descend into my music

     o mighty warrior

       delight

         let it be as air
             which billows in my hair

ruth

i had to go
even then i knew it
        one must do what one must…
after all   a relative is a relative

        how could she leave and live alone
        i, too,
                was facing all that solitary time to come but
        for her it would have been so hard…

i heard her worrying months ago
nothing special
        just bread crumbs between the too quiet
        and the talking late into the night
once
        she even said—
                i'd make a will
but i have nothing to leave but a few cooking pots
it was after that i thought
who would change her sheets if she were ill
or confront the landlord demanding rent she couldn't pay

        our return was a journey of compassion…

        for life like bitter herbs
                made me need her loneliness

hannah

he was always a talker—heaven knows...
how he talked my father into this marriage
i'll never understand
        and talk he did
                i'm sure of that
of course i came along
often dazzled with his dizzy words
and dizzy with the dazzle in his arms
             but now
can you imagine...
        that little hag and her little brood
pats me on the shoulder
        relax she says
        maybe when the moon is full
        but him i could choke
        cheer up it's not so bad
        after all you've got me
            ain 't that enough
        and he turns to walk away

even so

        the dazzle is there
        and the dizzy still sings in my ear

king david's mother

beautiful boy...
my beautiful, beautiful boy...
i could not have asked for better—
the last among my handsome sons

yet, it was *his* heart i could not read
as only a mother reads her sons
    the others wore their secrets in their faces

but his...
could even God read such a heart
and was He struck
at the sight of my beautiful boy
        my beautiful
            beautiful boy

wife of king saul

ours was a relationship of futility
he would never share how he felt
    yet he often wept because of david's songs
        then tears sharpened into madness
        like the spear he used
            to chase the shadow
                    he could not name

bathsheba

my hands will be as eyes
        that watch an evening unthrone my king

everything is ready

        like a bath prepared

the rape of tamar: ten years later

the shame could not kill
yet it became my grave
better had i died
the years in each moment whispered

his death was as simple
                as his lust
                soured into hate...

then my father turned away

now for a heart—

    ashes and a tomb

absalom's wife

perhaps nothing could be said for vanity
and yet
those glistening curls

with the wind brushing his hair black
he hung
as if trapped
by some other woman
tangled in her arms

rizpah whose name means *a hot stone*

my name
is the weary rock of sackcloth sorrow
        hot with my tears
i sit in the stench and price of atonement:
the death of my sons and my grief is their burial
each day fighting the buzzards is a strange justice
    like my name
if that's all i have then it will be mine
    until the rains wash me away

abishag the shunammite

his skin bruised as easily as lilies
          his breath was stale
                    death lingered in his lungs
so why do i weep for him—
                    this warrior with his ten thousands slain
                    each echoed in a fragile pulse
          beneath the shivering flesh
i, too, shivered when they first brought me here
   to blanket his tallow body with my warmth
the king is far away and very old—
          that
                    was common knowledge in my village
                    yet here i am
                              and so i weep
                                        for legends die
                                             like other men

the judgment of solomon: a woman in the crowd reflects

he's just a child . . .

    a child whose riddle
           is a wisdom unto himself
  we, the foolish ones
      seek answers where there are none

a jewish girl advises the wife of naaman

if only my master would go to the prophet...
    teasing
she called my outburst *just a bit of thunder before the rain*
    later i overheard them talk
        i even helped the others pack his things
        with questions thrilling in my ears
        what made her listen
        what made him go
            was it more than a snowy face and hands
            as i watched him leave
            she sighed
                    longing is much harder than disease

judith: widow

wit was his passion
well, at least one of them
but i suppose his real passion was life
    he would talk to me of it often and more
often he would listen i told him once he could
have been a teacher

 i fold his clothes to give away

 yet what man could wear his shoes

       fold, refold, and fold again

     somehow
         wisdom
         even now

esther: mystery

the king,
how could he not see, not hear...
    what has left him clueless
    to my voice
        my face and hands
was it his pride, his loss of face then shame
    or does he not want to see...
i feel like a doll—washed and dressed these passed months
    a treasured toy
    yet i am here
    and he does not see even when he looks
        and when he does
     i know how other i am

wild lady wisdom

they bought me a one way ticket
to somewhere to nowhere
after they thought they had tamed me
      but i will return
      to somewhere everywhere's downtown
pushing my cart
wearing my coat
         pushing my cart on the street
       to the corner
        shouting
            listen to me

gomer, wife of hosea

marriages are often tangled affairs
like vines overgrown, dying
    i, a wife he could not control
    became his shame
now in the buying back
i wear my silence and honor's claim

...was the Word...

mary

one of the women mentioned it today
    among the hours of stone beating grain
    and then she laughed
    child your time will come
     when you will also feel
              the darkest brush of wings
              like tiny moths or butterflies

              she laughed again
              imagine my surprise

the slaughter of the innocents

evening breezes cradle them...
rocking back and forth
the women of bethlehem know

anna, the prophetess: the presentation in the temple

we, like old books, were there——waiting
        we the foolish old
    always waiting like dried yellowed pages
        almost as foolish as the young
                coming to return their gift

mary: the child is found in the temple

what am i to make of His passion—
this intense child of mine...
all my words, like mirrors,
reflecting both surprise and treasure

elizabeth

a friend heard him speak
a voice in the wilderness
      crying out
            that's what she told me

  i sit
      looking out the window
      more like a curtain in the breeze
      that's how he danced once

the mother of peter and andrew

they're gone

both of them

like moths to a candle

i'm alone now in this bare room
needing some light

the wife of nicodemus

hours sit on their hands between the meals i serve   once
    there were questions, friends, and even strangers
    who brightened my table at supper
    as well as the times he went out at night
    to check the latest rumor of the coming messiah
    what was it he said, o yes,
        the wind blows where it chooses
    now the hours sit on their hands between the meals i serve...

peter's mother-in-law

rock, humph!
mark my words...
     and all he would do was laugh
and i'd get so frustrated from his teasing
     i'd have to leave the room
he would bait his hook for another nibble
     which i may add
he always got

the wife of matthew

soon after the wedding
our lives became a ledger
a daily counting
a mere series of columns and figures
he worked hard
until i wondered how much would be enough
then
everything unraveled
like a thread from my spindle
all because of *follow Me*

widow of naim

always
      it seemed unfinished
      that business of ours
      to be poor was bad enough
      until he wouldn't work
      and before that   it was just pieces of work
                                          here
            there
                    here again
                    so
      even before he died
      unfinished business was all i had
      but tomorrow i will walk behind another kind of death
            another kind of business
                    the kind i paid in widow's mites
            why shouldn't i grieve
            that is my wealth
                    to weep
                              and weep
                    and
                              weep

mary magdalene

how often i have heard them murmur—
        she's the one
even now, my family, what's left of them
        is still not used to the stares, the whispers...

        yet, how could i mind
                after all, He heard an inner music
                        beneath my demonic din—
                                the amazing sound of holy fire and wind

wife of jairus

feed her
was His last word on it
i stood there
gawking
silence like a restful sleep
broken
i awoke
fed beyond my wildest dreams

the woman with the hemorrhage

i was tired of their pity and their prayers
now for how many years
i saw their looks, their helpless silence...
    i'm so sorry drove me to distraction
until they learned my shame would last
perhaps forever
        then they disappeared like frightened children
            and the very thing they could not give
took all my courage...
        a touch so dark with breath
        gave back the power to make me whole

daughter of herodias
a.k.a. salome

i am my mother's daughter
   and because i am
i know his weakness...
  how i will toy with it
and when i do—
that will be worth far more than half a kingdom

the daughter of the canaanite woman

like a dog, a bone
  was the scrap he meant
        for hope to gnaw like teeth
                only to be buried
                and to rise again
                tit for tat in laughter

the woman caught in adultery

betrayed
i wear my sorrow like skin
    my elbows crossed as a corpse

i stand
condemned to a misery of silence
a world tilting on my shoulder
punished to carry it like death
from voices like stones

martha

what it boils down to
        the pantry
        the broom closet
        the kitchen
is everything in its place

           children pick up your toys
don't eat   you'll spoil your appetite
children do need order   don't they
and who would look after them, if not i

when all is said and done
there's nothing wrong with wanting
a well-run household, is there

mary, lazarus' sister

when he came back to us
his cheeks flamed white
his eyes tight from darkness
he talks so little now
each word measured
he listens
and he waits
in a shroud of reasons all his own

woman bent with infirmity

unnamed,
 i was less than servant animals
    voiceless in their grazing or being
    led to water
on the fringes
  i carried what they would have me be

 now called daughter of abraham, at last

        i am faithful *and* free

prodigal's mother

while against the window watching
foolish i know
i catch myself
and over little things
far too small for him to notice
until i cry
and he says, *what's wrong*
oh, nothing
just small things
like buttons i saved to mend
my younger son's favorite shirt
then my older son merely works and eats
never says any more to his father than he has to
and he takes it
what father wouldn't
he says

one of Jesus' female companions comments on
    the rich young man

like a child with his toys
you could not leave what owned
your well-ordered life of no surprises
    go, sell what you own and give it to the poor
was too simple for the answer
you will always be looking for

mother of the sons of zebedee

now that i think about it—
initiative would have been a better word
surely He would have understood that
    my husband wouldn't get excited even about the idea
            of meeting Him
        and i—well
            don't get me wrong
            one must act when opportunity knocks...
        we didn't get to our position
            without the help of some good timing on my part
            and we surely didn't stay there without
                    knowing somebody who knows somebody
        after all, these are hard times, you know
        as a result, a little foresight doesn't hurt...
        that i figured he would have understood

mary speaks after the death of joseph

just days after the brush fire
the fever came
burning itself out with death...
he, too, was my treasure—
he loved beyond the reach of words
that embraced the beckoning of dreams
such was our secret
such was our life

a woman who took yeast

He was good at telling stories...

i'm the one who took yeast
and three measures of flour
then made bread...
  it doesn't take much to tell a story:
  a beginning, a middle, and an end
  but His stories...
            He would let them be themselves
            like my yeast—
                    nothing else and nothing less

a woman at the last supper

        i knew exactly what He meant
            for i know about body and blood
    as well as flowers and yeast and sewing
    He used words i could understand about giving life
        and during those moments
            i felt the world revolved around me instead of only men

    but now
        there are dishes to wash, a floor to sweep
            and food to put away
                yes, i know about body and blood; about giving life
                and i will remember

veronica wipes the face of Jesus

it was a hard befriending
a sadness stretched out like cloth...
the world in His face
the face in all our seeking

a woman standing at a distance

now
  my sons are as nameless as i am—
as if they both had died in their leaving
    solitary, the cost...
      the cup, He called it
  silence   sorrowful as herbs in salt
  nameless as a woman and her sons

women who helped to bury Jesus

our alabaster jars carried our grief
what will we do with them
when they are empty, i asked
this same perfume
clinging to the shroud
our faces and hands

the road to emmaus

today he decides to walk
    this husband of mine—
     restless
    we talk all the way
    the way grievers do
under the burden of absence
suddenly words are not enough and i am silent
       words are not enough and he talks on
until
    absence breaks like bread into presence
    our sleepwalking wakes
     now our eyes burn
      everything new

thomas' twin sister

that's my brother for you
  so i'm not surprised with his comment
          unless i put my finger…
                  but his comments
                      were the questions he couldn't ask
  and   like me
        his buried longing rose…

mother of john the evangelist

once upon a time
            wrapped in nursery rhymes
            i cradled this child of mine

                        now
                          my lanky teen washes feet
                        i'm happy, he said

an early disciple ponders the story of jairus

       i, as a woman
have often wondered...
         who was this man, this father
        who loved a child—a girl
and who was this child
whose difficult dying sent him
on the wildest of journeys
theirs was a story buried beneath questions
i wish i could ask—
        concerning
a child who was loved as if she were a son
 and a father who loved because she was his child

lydia: the dealer in purple goods

i took his business and ran with it
        making good even better
            then voted best of best
        now
my profit margin is more than good risk management...
        an investment called everything

slave girl cured

when i sold bits of the future
my words always fell out like coins
yet words were also my prison
   the chains i could not silence
     and so i rattled on
       until his words voiced the earthquake
         for my escape

lady hope's riddle

i am today as well as tomorrow

i am the whisper in the shimmering silence:
        this is the secret you have been longing for
        yet did not know— until now

the woman who washed Jesus' feet:
resurrection monologue

the ones who were almost gentle were the boys
terrified at my perfume

i would have to bend and tie the shoes
of the older ones

but they were boys too

some in their anger

others—quick, sure—
noiseless in their leaving

i watched them all go
like leaves at the approach
of wind

i still wonder

there was more fragrance in my
tears
and sorrow in my hair...

more than i gave
to any man

epilogue: now, as i approach sixty

instead of purple,
   i shall wear autumn like silk
    and this wild, aching earth will
    fragrance my hair
  in the cool evening...

   the breeze, my holy lover, will whisper
   secrets...

with his gift of sunlight
      he will diamond my throat and wrists
        then
      as i dance
my shawl will flame out orange
      and red—
      and i shall toss jewels like
      leaves

   the breeze, my holy lover, will whisper
   secrets...

as for my leaving—
    i, with my own secret, will
walk barefoot
    into the coming night

NOTES

In the beginning...

creation: the Spirit speaks
>genesis 1:1-2

the name *woman* speaks to those who are abused
>genesis 2:23

bone of my bones and flesh of my flesh
>genesis 2:18-25

eve: the tree of knowledge
>genesis 3:1-6

eve's lament
>genesis 4:1-16

sarah
>genesis 12

lot's daughter speaks about her mother
>genesis 19:12-26

lot's daughter
>genesis 19:30-38

hagar
>genesis 21:14-21

sarah talks to isaac
>   genesis 22:1-19

rebekah
>   genesis 25:19-25

rachel
>   genesis 28:10-22, 29:15

leah
>   genesis 29-30

miriam, the prophetess, dances with her people at the red sea
>   exodus 15:20-21
>>   in memory of miriam, dear friend

rahab: prostitute of jericho
>   joshua 2:1-21

the wife and daughter of jephthah
>   judges 11:34-40

delilah's song
>   judges 16:4-31

ruth
>   ruth 1:1-18

hannah
>   1 samuel 1:1-18

king david's mother
>   1 samuel 16:12

wife of king saul
    1 samuel 17
bathsheba
    2 samuel 11:1-5

the rape of tamar: ten years later
    2 samuel 13:1-19

absalom's wife
    2 samuel 18:9-15

rizpah whose name means *a hot stone*
    2 samuel 21:1-14

abishag the shunammite
    1 kings 1:1-4

the judgment of solomon: a woman in the crowd reflects
    1 kings 3:16-28

a jewish girl advises the wife of naaman
    2 kings 5:1-19

judith: widow
    judith 8:1-8

esther: mystery
    esther 2:1-18

wild lady wisdom
    proverbs chapter 1

gomer, wife of hosea
    hosea 1-3:2

...*was the Word*...

mary
> luke 1:26-38

the slaughter of the innocents
> matthew 2:16-19

anna, the prophetess: the presentation in the temple
> luke 2:36-38
>> "the love of God is folly"
>> —a french saying

mary: the child is found in the temple
> luke 2:41-51

elizabeth
> luke 1:42-45, 3:3-6

the mother of peter and andrew
> john 1:40-42

the wife of nicodemous
> john 3:1-21

peter's mother-in-law
> luke 4:38-39

the wife of matthew
> matthew 9:9-13

widow of naim
> luke 7:11-17

mary magdalene
> luke 8:2-3

wife of jarius
> luke 8:40-56

the woman with the hemorrhage
> luke 8:40-48

daughter of herodias a.k.a. salome
> matthew 14:3-12

the daughter of the canaanite woman
> matthew 15:21-28

the woman caught in adultery
> john 8:3-11

martha
> luke 10:38-42

mary, lazarus' sister
> john 11:1-14

woman bent with infirmity
> luke 13:10-17

prodigal's mother
> luke 15:11-32

one of Jesus' female companions comments on the
rich young man
> matthew 19:17-22
>> "love defines the letting go"

mother of the sons of zebedee
>matthew 20:20-28

a woman who took yeast
>luke 13:20-21

a woman at the last supper
>mark 14:22-25

a woman standing at a distance
>matthew 27:55-56

women who helped to bury Jesus
>luke 23:55-24:4

the road to emmaus
>luke 24:13-35

thomas' twin sister
>john 20:24-29

the woman who washed Jesus' feet: resurrection
monologue
>luke 7:38-50

mother of john the evangelist
>john 13:1-15

an early disciple ponders the story of jairus
>luke 8:40-56

lydia: the dealer in purple goods
>acts 16:11-15

slave girl cured
> acts 16:16-18

lady hope's riddle
> 1 corinthians 13:13

In Gratitude

I would like to thank my religious community, the Sisters of the Incarnate Word and Blessed Sacrament, for allowing me the time to write.

Thanks to Tom Lombardo, my editor, who challenged me to write.

Rabbi Ruth Langer who told me that my midrash was just good as anyone else's midrash and suggested I write a piece on Leah.

Barbara Morikawa who read the manuscript with her meticulous eye for details.

Sandra Senecal who encouraged me to be ready for an opportunity.

Pam Edwards who shared with me the ups and downs of being a writer.

Jewell Shaw who listened.

Elizabeth Whitlow for her love of words.

Leslie McLaurin for being herself.

Virginia Cowen, teacher.

Thanks to all the women of the Bible who were instrumental in shaping this manuscript: I hope I have expressed at least a small measure of your true voices.

Sister Lou Ella Hickman

Sister Lou Ella Hiskman is a member of the Sisters of the Incarnate Word and Blessed Sacrament of Corpus Christi, Texas. She has a master's in theology and she taught on all levels, including college. She has worked in two libraries before working in a parish. Presently, she is a freelance writer as well as a certified spiritual director. Her poems and articles have been published in numerous magazines, including *After Shocks: Poetry of Recovery for Life-Shattering Events*, edited by Tom Lombardo, and in *Down the Dark River*, edited by Philip Kolin.

Cover artist SISTER MARILYN SPRINGS is a member of the Sisters of the Incarnate Word and Blessed Sacrament of Corpus Christi, Texas. Sister Marilyn was born in Buffalo, New York, and later attended college at Our Lady of the Lake University in San Antonio, Texas, where she earned a Bachelor of Arts degree. She later earned a Master's degree in Catholic School Leadership from St. Mary's University in San Antonio, Texas. Sister Marilyn has been painting for over 35 years, and has taught art in elementary, middle school, and high school levels. She specializes in portraits of women and children of color. The medium she prefers to paint with is acrylic because of the vibrant colors. Sister Marilyn is currently the principal at Incarnate Word Academy in Brownsville, Texas.

CPSIA information can be obtained at www.ICGtesting.com
Printed in the USA
BVOW08s0548050915

416534BV00001B/1/P